WE DON'T NEED NO STINKIN' CONSULTANTS

Using Business Improvement Consultants

When, Why, How, and If

NANCY KRUG

WE DON'T NEED NO STINKIN' CONSULTANTS
Using Business Improvement Consultants
When, Why, How, and If

Practical Leadership Strategies

Printed in the United States of America
First Printing 2020
First Edition 2020

10 9 8 7 6 5 4 3 2 1

WE DON'T NEED NO STINKIN' CONSULTANTS

Table of Contents

Introduction

I wrote this book partly because I wish I'd had a book like this to read when I was working as a consultant.

Back then, in the 1980's, I had limited business experience and didn't want to make mistakes, especially the public or expensive kinds. I was surrounded by many intimidatingly smart and experienced people, and I had a thousand questions, plus thousands more I didn't even know how to ask.

In addition to watching and learning, I wanted some quick reading. So, this being before Amazon.com, I mail ordered stuff from Jossey-Bass and scoured physical book stores and the local library for knowledge – and salvation.

What I found were massive books, or books full of theory, or books where I had to painstakingly find and extract the hidden bits of knowledge that I would need in 12 hours, on Monday morning.

Often I yearned for just the damn answers, or an outline of the right questions.

So maybe you are reading this because on Monday you need to make a decision, or a presentation, or have a new direction. I've carved the word count down so you can read quickly, but more importantly, use my words as fuel for thought and inspiration for action.

Please skim, or skip, or diligently plow through the whole thing. Whatever gets you to find a way to move ahead, with outside help or not.

I do believe strongly that good consulting with a good client can do amazing things, under the right conditions. This book briefly describes those things:

1. Good consulting: what it looks like

2. Good client: what that means

3. Right conditions: what they are

By extension, without one or more of those things, you might have trouble, or failure with consultants, and might be better off alone if that situation stays the same.

There are lots of books about consultants and consulting. Some are very good. You may want to read them later. In the meantime, I hope a brief introduction will give you new perspectives, and maybe afterwards you can decide if you need another book, or a good consultant. Or both.

Acknowledgements

This book owes its existence to some wonderful people in my life, who took the time to read and re-read the drafts and tell me when my baby was too ugly to expose to the reading public.

1. My sister Loraine Fick, whose constant encouragement and insightful editing made all the difference.
2. My friend Kris Maegli, who, as a client team member, taught me a lot about business and excellence.
3. My husband Woody Owen, whose support is all I could wish for.
4. Woody's close friend Bob Gault, whose vast experience in business added useful perspective to the book.
5. Woody's dear friend Gerald Woodard, who critiqued an early draft so helpfully.
6. A large number of people in my business life who contributed to the rich and often rewarding experiences that inspired this book.

Is this book for you?

This book is aimed at the company decision maker(s). That person (or persons) needs to approve the intervention of a business consultant, and/or lead the consulting project. The target reader comes with a substantial foundation of knowledge and experience in business management, and this book seeks to build upon that foundation.

Everyone in the company, however, can get information on consulting and consultants from this book. Even after a consultant is okayed to start work, this book can provide direction on how to work with them and get the best from them.

So, if it's entirely your call to make about hiring, or if you just need to find a way to work with an invading horde, there is something here for you.

Section A: Deciding

Chapter 1

Change is hard

You know change and managing change is difficult if you have ever tried either. Changing even just your own behavior is a challenge: changing the behaviors of a group of others is hugely difficult even in the best of circumstances. The difficulties can be even greater depending on company age, culture, and the management style and skill.

This is a bit like sketching out a plan for world peace on one page: many excellent books exist on this subject. So just for starters:

1. **Change is harder work than not-change.** And we all have limited energy.
2. **Change requires motivation.** Not-change can skip motivation.
3. **Change requires direction.** Not-change already has one.
4. **Change in one thing often requires change in many things.** Limited control and energy interfere.
5. **Change involves more apparent risk of failure** than not-change.

The change manager has to understand, address and overcome all of these challenges.

And to paraphrase W. Edwards Deming, the 20th century quality improvement guru, improvements have to be made systematically and be led by a knowledgeable leader who understands that business problems are typically systemic, or management, or process problems, not worker problems.

The first step in making change, then, is evaluating your company's ability to overcome the barriers to change.

Chapter 2

Signs your company needs a consultant

Every company has problems and needs to change. Not every problem or change calls for outside help, of course.

Nevertheless, there are some important signs that outside help is worth considering.

1. **Problems never seem to get fixed**. Problems persist unchanged despite attempts to correct them. Problems persist with no attempt to correct them. Problems are brushed off even when they seriously affect customers, revenue, and employees. Promised changes from senior management routinely do not occur.

2. **Key business measures are on a persistent downward slide**: revenues, turnover, market share, customer satisfaction, employee retention.

3. **Simmering frustration and anger,** and/or despair, and/or apathy, seem to be the prevailing employee attitude.

4. **Your folks do not have a clear idea on how to fix** important problems, whether organizational problems or narrower technical problems.

5. Problems need to be solved but **your people are completely out of time and energy**.
6. Worthy business opportunities float by and disappear because **people are too stretched**.
7. Worthy business opportunities float by and disappear because your **company doesn't have the right skills, priorities, energy**…you name it.
8. Your most valued and respected **customers say "you are getting it all wrong."**
9. You see **a steady departure of your best people**, who tell you the same things over and over: what needs to be fixed, and how those things fueled their departure.
10. Your **stockholders and investors** tell you, with a serious look, that you need to make some changes.
11. You see **online comments and reviews** rating your company below your competitors and peers.
12. Your **senior management micromanages** more and more, in an (apparently frantic) attempt to right the ship.

There are more. The theme is: **persistent and continuing problems that don't get better.**

Comparing your company to others is one way to get clarity on your firm's situation. We have all seen the seemingly unstoppable slide of companies that could not change fast enough:

- American Motors
- Digital Equipment
- Kodak
- Kmart
- Sears
- Blockbuster
- Buggy whip manufacturers

Do you see your company more like them or less? How? Can you select companies that do change well and see how much alike or different your company is to them?

While the focus in this book is on solving problems, many of the same techniques used to solve problems can facilitate pursuing opportunities. But mostly this book will be about solving the problems of the company that is on fire – in a bad way.

Chapter 3

Signs your company can change itself

You and your organization can make needed change fast and effectively enough alone if:

1. **You know what needs to change**.

   This is extremely important and must include both the apparent problems and the root causes. For instance, if your revenue is tanking, your product development, hiring practices, and/or management style could be part of the problem's scope.

2. **You know how to create organizational change effectively; with lasting results and continual improvement into the future**.

   An effective change process would include a clear, practical, actionable project plan with people, product, and process elements, timelines, resource needs, communication plans, and objectives that address root causes.

3. **You have the resources to lead, manage, and execute change, and those resources know what to do**. Those people also have the authority they need.

Depending on your organization's experience with driving change, you have on hand the top level and working level people who can develop and execute a detailed roadmap for the improvements your firm needs.

4. **You have the priority on change that is needed**. This includes being able to assign skilled and valuable people to the mission.

   You know that significant change isn't a part time job for all of your folks: some additional people need a greater focus and additional work hours to keep the energy and forward movement going. You know that those full-time people cost money and you are committed to paying for their important roles.

5. **The people who call the shots strongly support a change process and have a clear vision of what needs to change.**

   The top brass, including you, are not sniping, undercutting, sabotaging, devaluing, shaving budgets, destaffing, or expecting unreasonably fast results for unreasonably low investments. All key decision makers understand the scope, objectives, costs, and risks and are in regular communication on objectives, efforts, results, and course corrections.

6. **Politics don't interfere.**

   Your company's leadership has the will to drive success, support change efforts, and stamp out destructive politics. Maybe someone wants the project to fail, or wants your group to fail, or wants to use the project money somewhere else. When power comes with politics, it can overwhelm the positive things set in motion to improve your company.

7. **Your organization is able to contribute ideas, energy, and time to change.**

   There are people in your organization who know what needs to be different and better, and they have the time and skills to bring those ideas to life among their co-workers. Perhaps new hires have brought industry knowledge with them, or your firm has invested in continuous education programs. Perhaps you already have some skilled people with fulltime organizational change responsibilities.

8. **After you fix today's problems, you know there will be others soon after.**

   You know it's not "one and done." You have funding not just for this time around but as an ongoing line item. Your organization is always looking for the next problem or opportunity to work on.

9. **You ensure that your organization learns more change and improvement skills, and ensure they make continuous improvement a normal part of their job.**

   Your organization – at all levels – is learning all the time.

10. **You have enough calendar time.**

    In your current situation, your firm has the people and process to keep your business alive and thriving in the face of what is currently going on. You don't need more time or money and you are not desperate for emergency changes.

You may conclude that these points are true enough for your firm. In particular, they are true enough to make and/or keep your firm nimble, profitable, growing, and a great place to work.

In addition, there are **very good alternatives to using consultants.**

1. **Hire or assign one or more fulltime continuous improvement specialists** who report high in the organization. Make it their job to respond to key senior management concerns and priorities, and to identify other issues worthy of significant improvement efforts. Allow them the time, resources, and authority to start and run projects and implement improvements.

Encourage and address their concerns about the organization and their ability to change it.

2. **Create a senior management team** responsible for identifying and pursuing significant change efforts within the company. Require accountability and energetically follow up on a routine basis.

3. **Implement bottom-up communication channels** to identify and resolve issues seen and experienced by all levels and functions within the organization. Some may need to be anonymous. Be sure to have some feedback mechanism so input doesn't feel like it is going into a black hole. Be prepared to act on information you receive: total inaction will discourage future input.

4. **Examine your management team fiercely**, looking for levels of knowledge and energy in change creation. Anyone dragging feet? Wimping out on dealing with performance problems? Or anyone with pent-up energy to create change?

5. **Create a learning environment** by training yourself and having regular training and learning opportunities for your organization. Focus on the basics first and often, such as these:

    a) **Meeting management**: not trivial, it is the basis for group problem solving, including having a solid agenda, a facilitator, decision makers, note takers, concrete next steps, time management, and so on.

b) Fundamentals for **group problem solving**: flow charting, value stream analysis, brainstorming, flipchart listing, effective breakout groups, and more.

c) Fundamentals of **quality control**, six sigma, and other time tested process improvement tools. Be careful of getting more technical than is useful within each work group, however.

d) **Learning as a constant process**, not a special project.

e) **Skill implementation immediately after training**. Classes are wasted unless quickly used.

f) **Management fads**: be skeptical and wary. They may have merit but can be viewed wrongly as silver bullets. Fundamentals come first.

g) **Train managers** as well as workers. Don't skip levels.

Chapter 4

Signs your company cannot change itself

While in the long run your company **should** be able to change and improve itself, in the immediate future a consultant can jump start and/or accelerate this process when one or more of these situations exist:

1. **You do NOT know what needs to change.**

   This means your organization does not have a way to move from symptoms to the real problems, and your organization does not know how to systematically look at systems and processes to identify all of the flaws. Your organization also does not have a clear mission that drives what is important enough to focus change upon. And if a LOT of things need to change, you do not know how to attack such a big tangle without destroying your people or your company.

2. **You do NOT know how to create organizational change effectively; with lasting results and continual improvement into the future**.

   Here, your organization does not know how to prioritize problems that are uncovered, how to address problems systematically, how to create a habit of continuous improvement, or how to educate all people in the organization in change management. Further, your organization does not systematically address the flip side: business opportunities.

3. **You do NOT have the resources to lead, manage, and execute change, and/or those resources do not know how to do it.**

   Your organization does not have people who have specific, specialized change management skills or who are directed to use those skills, or who have the time to use those skills.

4. **You do NOT have the priority on change that is needed.**

   Change is not treated as top priority but more as a side job that is dealt with when all other activities are taken care of. Skilled and valuable people are not assigned to lead and staff the effort as their primary responsibility.

5. **The people who call the shots do NOT strongly support a change process and do not have a clear vision of what needs to change.**

   Senior management does not uniformly see the changes needed or acknowledge the cost of making those changes.

6. **Politics DO interfere.**

When people see threats to security, status, pay, or prestige they may act in ways that block or damage improvement efforts. Maybe there is competition for a promotion, or a deep personality clash. Maybe someone influential just hates to hear that they may be wrong or that there is a better way. In any of these cases, leadership cannot or will not deal effectively with the situation or the damage caused.

7. **Your organization CANNOT contribute ideas and energy to change.**

   Your employees do not feel free to bring up ideas or feel encouraged to contribute to the company's well-being. Or, your folks do not have much to input, due to any number of causes.

8. **You do NOT have enough calendar time.**

   You are running out of survival time, and have little available resource time to apply to your problems while still executing day to day.

9. **You do NOT have ways to get honest and complete information about each of the issues above.**

   Senior executives like you live in an information-restricted environment, and you do not have good sources, good data or effective conduits for figuring out what is going on in useful detail in your company.

Chapter 5

Knowing WHY a consultant can contribute

If your organization has no experience working with consultants, it is entirely reasonable to wonder what is so special about them. How can they do that which you cannot?

It is not because a consultant is smarter than you are.

Seriously. A useful and effective consultant doesn't need to be smarter than the smart people in your organization. They can't be dim, of course. What they do have is specialized knowledge and experience in using it.

That's pretty much it. If your organization needed an accountant, or a nuclear engineer, they wouldn't say "Oh, we can just wing it with the staff we already have in materials management."

It may be unconsciously assumed that change management, from design to execution, is something anyone can do just like breathing: no school or experience required.

Actually, the skills needed to get an organization's people and leaders to change how things are done are extensive. As for strategies for change: there will be a few effective ones, but also a zillion ways to mess things up. Finding the few effective strategies is key. Having assistance from people who have already found effective strategies can be invaluable.

As you consider the challenges that face your company, you may be ready to think about the additional challenge of finding a person or company who can understand your organization's culture, mission, problems, root causes, people, and processes, and who then can manage the improvement of the business in a way that fosters continuous change and improvement after he/she is gone.

That significant challenge may seem insurmountable and get you to rethink things: maybe your firm can indeed do it yourselves, even while you continue your full-time jobs.

Although…that full-time job thing does make it seem a bit harder. And it's not just workload, but focus.

Chapter 6

Knowing WHAT a consultant can contribute

In the last chapter, I said that an effective consultant brings special skills and knowledge. What does that mean, more precisely?

1. **Consultants know that every system or process can be designed and studied systematically**. Consultants also know specific methods for doing this. These methods are not necessarily high tech, either: some involve paper and markers and sticky notes. Consultants know that every process now done by seat-of-pants has already been designed elsewhere to be systematic and reliable, and your company can quickly graduate to that more effective level without extensive trial and error.

2. **Consultants are experienced and trained in knowing which systems companies need in order to be capable**. These systems include, for instance, which communications are typically effective, and which management measurements work best. Creating strategies, managing meetings, and many other business processes have been created already by consultants and need not be re-developed from scratch by your company.

3. **People are part of every company**, sharing the same wants, needs, fears, and issues. The same approaches work to improve people issues regardless of industry, and consultants may have the formal organizational development and human resources training to offer new options.
4. **Consultants have seen success and failure in many companies and know what is possible and what creates failure**. The signs are there in every company, and experienced consultants can spot the signs quickly for both success and failure. I call it "bugs and worms:" look in the same approximate places and find the same nasty critters in most companies. (The positive signs are also similar in many cases.)
5. **Consultants have seen what systems and processes work and don't work** in similar companies, as well as in those apparently very different. Those lessons can be shared much more quickly than learning them from scratch. For instance, bottling lines work very much the same in beer and in photochemical businesses. Sales methods and systems may be very similar among large equipment businesses in completely different industries.
6. **Consultants know how to work with every level of an organization**. Even more importantly, they are free to do so, not being bound by an organization's culture or protocol, or fears of career suicide. A consultant can

"talk dirty" if done diplomatically and strategically, and still get paid.

There are other reasons for using a consultant beyond skills, however. The consultant arrangement puts pressure on a company to achieve change objectives in other ways:

1. The **"Power of the Invoice"** means that the senior managers who see a weekly or monthly invoice from consultants, along with their expenses, feel they need to get something for their money. These managers will be anxious to ensure consultants can do their job.

2. **Consultants add more manpower** to the change process – dedicated manpower. What's more, this manpower knows what to do from the beginning, and this manpower does not have another fulltime job to deal with.

3. **Outsiders are noteworthy** and notable: their involvement generates interest and a break from routine for the organization. Those employees who most thrive on change and improvement are more able to contribute. Outsiders generate excitement (which needs to be managed to be positive versus negative).

4. **Consultants can be a positive political tool** when managers wish to visibly demonstrate that they are putting extraordinary effort into improvement. The

intended audience might be, say, corporate senior management or regulatory bodies.

5. **Consultants can unearth hidden personnel gems** and both use and promote their talents and contributions: that accounts payable clerk with the eye for finding spending waste, or the production person with ideas for rapid product changeover.

6. **Managers at all levels have imperfect and incomplete information**: the higher, the more filtered. Access to all levels of people in your organization (if accompanied by trust) allows consultants to find and share important real-world information from the trenches with the leaders who can change things.

Chapter 7

Knowing WHEN to consider help from a consultant

Some situations make using a consultant easier, or help make good outcomes more likely.

1. **When you are newish to the job**, but after enough evaluation to see the scope and type of problems to be solved. This makes it evident that the consultant is a resource like many others, but that the problems can be solved faster or more effectively with extra troops.
2. **When an urgent situation arises**, such as:

- Product recall
- Tumbling stock price
- Factory burns down
- Employee fatality
- Environmental disaster
- Critical change in competitive landscape

3. **When a big change or development occurs**, such as:

- A new business is acquired
- A customer schedules a major inspection that you are not ready for

- A major contract requires important changes

4. **When visibly doing something different or extra is needed**, whether in the eyes of your people, your customers, your marketplace, or your government.
5. **When current business practices have allowed or enabled a consistent decline** in market share, business performance, employee retention, etc., and there is no sign of reversal.

Think ahead to the future, say, one year from now, and ask yourself a few questions.

1. Will it be easier or harder to justify and secure consulting help in the future versus now? Will doors be closed later on? Will questions arise about what took so long to make the call?
2. If your situation persists in a year, will you have time and resources then to work on it?

Even for a senior manager, using a consultant raises questions which can be easier to respond to when reasonable people can see the justification quickly. Since hiring consultants can create fear, resentment, and budget strain, having a clear reason for moving in that direction helps keep the working environment positive.

Section B: Doing

Chapter 8

Defining a project scope: toe dipping to whole hog

When you are first considering a consultant, very likely you have some areas of concern in mind for a project focus. However, the scope of the effort isn't fixed and unchangeable, and it may make sense to enlarge or shrink it based upon current conditions.

For instance, if you and/or your staff is highly skeptical and negative, or if you have significant budgetary limitations, or if you think you just need a small jump start or kick in the pants, then the project scope can be reduced in time, expected outcomes, and staffing.

In a more limited project, your staff learns to work with an outside resource while knowing that the interference will end soon. Other senior managers will see how the process works. In the meantime, everyone in your organization may have a chance to see a whole new way of working, including ways to examine, prioritize, and attack the otherwise bewildering and overwhelming current state.

A smaller scope project needs to be set up fairly, of course, with achievable objectives.

On the other hand, smaller scope projects use up time and resources that may delay other important work, or a smaller project may not address fundamentals comprehensively. Just think of project scope as one item to negotiate when discussing a consulting project, not a given.

Overlapping projects are another option, with longer and shorter projects running concurrently if not successively.

Your consulting project size and scope will depend on many factors. Your consultant will propose one option, but you get a vote too.

Here are some factors to consider:

1. **Culture**: Would you say your company was broadly hostile or broadly welcoming to a consulting project? Does it differ by group or level of management? Are there labor unions to work with? Are there any reasons to design short versus longer duration projects?

2. **Time**: Is there a specific deadline to achieve a specific objective? Are there any calendar periods to avoid or take advantage of? Are there any fiscal periods to accommodate? Is there a maximum time period available for a project?

3. **Funding**: What can you afford to spend? What is your company's tolerance for risk? Does your company need to see some proof of the consultant's ability to perform? Does the improvement work need to be rapid return or long-term payoff, or both, or neither?

4. **Other**: Are there any confidential situations driving scope and schedule (say, business sale or bankruptcy looming, etc.)? Do you need to demonstrate something quickly to prove the concept before moving to a larger project? Do you have personnel issues that you need third party analysis or help with? Other?

Here are some options that depend on your situation:

1. Consider a small project to start with, that demonstrates the consultant's capabilities and your company's abilities to work with consultants. If successful, it can reduce distrust and anxiety.
2. Consider a larger project with well defined "low hanging fruit" sub-projects. This not only can prove capabilities but also identify issues with the project set-up that can be corrected early. It also can create and maintain enthusiasm during a longer project timeframe.
3. Consider selecting the area of work using input by employees and other managers. Consider asking for volunteer managers, if that fits with your situation. Think about a long term with multiple projects, with or without consulting help.

Chapter 9

Finding and selecting consultants

Any specific consulting company I mention might change its nature by the time you read these words, so there will be no specific endorsements.

Also, any consulting company is the product of the people it employs. And while this is true of any company, the consultant company's culture will be more critical to you than if they were a manufacturer or even a typical service provider, because they will be getting far deeper into your private business during any consulting assignment.

Yes, size matters. If you are the leader of a Fortune 100 firm with a large scope need, inevitably you will need more resources.

There are very large firms: think Ernst & Young or McKinsey. There are midsize companies, "boutique" companies, and sole proprietorships. There are places (like Forbes) to use to get ratings on these companies. There also are other places to look to get background on a consultant, such as looking at the kind and number of jobs being advertised by each, or reading online reviews by employees.

As you find different firms to interview, however, the same steps to evaluation apply. What you are looking for is a company with integrity: willing to be specific, make reasonable and valuable promises, put them in writing, and agree to reasonable consequences/corrections for problems or failures.

From the first meeting with prospective consultants, your antenna should be up. Keep them up as things progress, since you will see changes in staffing as your consulting project goes from sales to analysis to project. Each of these stages will have different people whose strength is in those activities.

In the selection process, I hope you have others in your organization who can participate, and who can watch and independently evaluate the fit and value of each candidate you consider. It is important to have others with good "stink sniffers" who are unafraid to differ with you on their conclusions. As the senior person and the purse-string holder, you inevitably will get biased sales efforts, but your colleagues may see some realities differently from their points of view.

No matter which consultant(s) you are considering, what follow are some topics to consider as you evaluate who might be the best fit for your organization and its needs. This effort is similar to a job application process for a senior executive. (A non-disclosure agreement will make sense somewhere in this process: unlike a job applicant, your consultant will receive sensitive company information during even initial evaluation.)

As you evaluate different consulting people and companies, find out:

1. How well has this consultant performed before? Get references and actually consult them, in depth.

2. Has this consultant ever seen your industry before? Seen your problem before? What was learned? How were the issue(s) dealt with? If not, what similar situation might have been experienced?

3. Explain your hands-on involvement in important projects like this. How does the consultant feel about your veto power over individual staff? About your desire to interview each consultant coming on board? And your expectation to be closely involved in schedules, reporting, and results?

4. What is the process, exactly? Does the consultant feel comfortable going into details about time, money, contracts, and so on?

5. What is the strength or special skill of this consultant? Can they describe why they should be hired?

6. Will the consultant discuss fee structures, or dance around it until far down the pike? You have budgets and financial goals that need to be accommodated with

a special expense of a consultant rolled in. Too much handwaving and "not to worry" dismissals suggest either nasty surprise or ignorance.

7. Will this consultant discuss in general terms how an improvement project would be structured and what sorts of activities will be pursued? Specificity suggests knowledge; vagueness suggests seat of pants.

8. Are you the right size for this consultant? Large consultant firms want large projects with big fees, and smaller jobs with those firms will inevitably get lower skilled people and less attention. Large jobs may overwhelm the capabilities of small consulting companies. Ask your consultant being interviewed how they see your fit, but evaluate their answer critically. After all, if they are talking to you, they want a sale.

9. Is your project very specific or broad in scope? Very specific might be evaluating M&A (merger and acquisition) opportunities in your field. Broad might be overhauling your entire electric generator production business to meet competitive challenges. In each case, do you have the right specific or broad skill set in your consultant?

10. Show who you are in a positive way. Your consultant, if selected, will respond to that style. If you are reasonably demanding, insightful, analytical, observant, and a

good communicator, your consultant will go back to his/her firm and say "we are going to have to staff this job with our A team, because that executive will see right through any ringers and call us on it." If you are less demanding, even a consultant with integrity will find it easier to staff with new hires or B team people, and give your project less attention and quality.

And after all those questions, keep your antenna up to sense things like: do you get the impression that he/she/they think your business is beneath them? Do you hear hesitant promises, like they don't know how to address an issue but are sure they can figure it out on time? Do you sense an attitude of superiority? Do you smell bullshit? Do you hear irritation when you start to talk about limitations and consequences and measurable results? Do you feel dismissed or diminished rather than respected?

Watch yourself, too. Have you handed over all your power already, as if you are a suffering patient with a doctor, hoping for a miracle and afraid of asking challenging questions? On the other hand, have you treated the consultant with respect and without suspicious overtones? Have you hidden too well your style of reasonable expectations with thorough follow up?

Chapter 10

Exploratory discussions with possible consultants

No matter how you selected your consultant or short list of consultants, there are some things to look for in the final selection process.

1. Before talking in depth to any consultant, **knowing what you would like to improve** is important. Both good and bad consultants may want to change and/or expand the project scope: be prepared to decide if this is a good idea or if you feel a test run is more advisable, with future business possible.

2. During discussions, look **for clarity versus buzz words** and arrogance. Ask for clarification and be concerned if the tone ever deviates from respectful in their responses. Can they boil things down to clear and pithy, or do they stick to complex, convoluted explanations?

3. During the project, **don't turn over control** completely, either consciously or by neglect. Make that expectation clear from the outset.

4. There are **good consultants and bad ones**, good consulting companies and bad ones. You may not be able to tell right away. You need to think about what

would tell you the difference, at the start or along the way.

5. You will always need **performance expectations** and performance clauses in contracts.
6. You need clearly defined **expense policies** in contracts, including the right to oversight.
7. Consultants should be willing to **share their methods** with you, and be willing to help you live without their long-term involvement.
8. In advance, decide: are you lousy at giving **constructively worded negative feedback** to your employees or co-workers? That's a valuable skill, and one you will need in order to constructively work with your consultants. Suffering in silence will cost you in a consulting assignment, and if you have good consultants, they will want to know what they need to do to be effective.
9. In advance, decide: are you lousy at giving **positive constructive feedback**? Consultants are people too, often excited about success. You will get more from happy consultants. (Rather like employees, yes?)

Chapter 11

Bad consultants versus good consultants

I was a consultant and I admired many of my colleagues. But not all of them.

The most important thing as a client, I believe, is to not put up with bad consulting or bad consultants. Challenge the person or company to improve, and fast. Do not assume you have no power to select the individuals working with you or your company, or to specify and enforce performance expectations.

At the same time, don't take out your frustrated-dictator side on consultants. The ideal leader will treat consultants with the same respect and high expectations as he/she would (or should) do with their employees. The performance expectations for the consultant should be reasonably demanding, not super-human, since your own organization must be able to continue the work after the consultants are gone.

Further, what may look like bad consulting may instead be the doing of your own organization. Maybe your staff members fail to attend key meetings. Maybe agreed upon tasks are not completed. Consultants who actually implement change cannot do it to you, but must do it with you.

The **best consultants** are excellent people and assets. The excellent consultant:

1. Is interested in success and excellence. He/she is always learning from clients, and from reading and training.
2. Enjoys challenge and solving difficult problems.
3. Enjoys and stimulates smart people.
4. Works very hard.
5. Treats people with genuine respect, and displays no arrogance.
6. Enjoys and practices listening.

The excellent consultant not only gets the best from the organization and the project, but makes the people feel the best about the process and the outcome.

A **bad consultant** or consulting company can be bad for a number of reasons: personality, skill, or outcomes. The bad consultant:

1. Is dislikable. He/she may be arrogant, a poor listener, tone deaf to company culture, etc., but if the result is that you do not like him/her, you will be much less likely to get value from that person. Even if they are right.

2. Is lazy, relative to the invoice. No matter the invoice, however, failure to meet project requirements on time due to his/her own failure to exert reasonable efforts is a problem.
3. Is unskilled in the project's needs. For instance, larger consulting companies will staff projects with a mix of experienced and less-so people. If any consultant is unable to contribute as you would expect, this may be either a solvable problem (replace person) or a mark of bad faith by the consulting company.
4. Is "cookie cutter." This means that the consultant is trying to make a stock solution fit your specific but non-matching problem.
5. Is a bullshitter. If you cannot get straight talk and straight answers, this may be covering up other problems, or covering up a desire to foster long-term dependency, or worse.
6. Is not judicious with expense money. If you pay expenses, you have the right to specify what you will and won't reimburse for. Your consultant should care about managing your company's money frugally.
7. Costs too much. Whether apparently justified or not, some companies are just expensive. While cost by itself may not mean Bad Consultant, it might mean bad for your company. The big strategy companies come to

mind as costly, such as McKinsey: their fees can run into the multi-millions of dollars. (The fees may be entirely justifiable and worthwhile, by the way.) Smaller consulting companies will cost less. However, for any company, the estimated invoice should be scrutinized and challenged. Consulting companies know that the customer probably does not know what consulting should cost, or how big a project team should be, etc. You may need to exert your confidence to extract the answers you need to get a cost-effective project.

8. Does not keep promises. These promises can be for business confidentiality, project results, or other. You the client may be responsible for some shortcomings, but to the extent the consultant has fallen short without correction or acceptable explanation, they are bad.
9. Behaves unethically. This can be hiring away your good people, deliberately failing to work in the client's best interests, billing you while not working, and so on.

If you are a tough but fair client, you will get the best consultants and the best results. Those companies that do not insist on the best will not always get it.

Chapter 12

Controlling the contract and the project

There you are. You've just picked a consulting company after finding what you hope will be the best fit for your company. After several meetings, you sense they have a clear idea of how to proceed and have a lot of experience in projects like yours.

You are already exhausted: you hired these folks for a reason. You are tempted to say "you guys, just handle it, will ya, and tell me when you're done."

Don't do it.

What you really signed up for when you enlisted outside help was a lot more work, because they can't do it without you. Or, at least, they can't do it right and on budget without you. And what's more, if you are absentee, your company could be taken for a ride (I mean that in a bad way).

From beginning to end, you need to participate in and control:

1. **People**
2. **Schedule**
3. **Cost**
4. **Outcome**

The next four chapters will go into more detail on each of these, but the headlines are:

1. **People**: Know who your consultants are individually, expect excellence, and act on issues. Communicate with your employees who will be working closely with the consultants.
2. **Schedule**: Participate in creating a detailed schedule, review at least weekly, and act on issues immediately.
3. **Cost**: Create detail in the contract on allowable costs and how deviations will be handled. Review frequently with help of finance folks, hold people accountable, act on issues immediately.
4. **Outcome**: ensure measurable performance specificity is baked into the contract, including timeframes, and include consequences for failure and problems. Act on issues immediately.

If you are already doing similar things with your own organization – clear goals, follow up, and consequences – then you are miles ahead of the typical company. Treat your consultants like your valuable employees: respectfully but with high expectations.

However, if you are not one of those fortunate few, then you will need to bone up on your skills. Right away. Because bad things can happen if you don't.

Let me give you a scenario which I have seen happen. Your chosen consulting company is reputable, with good references and track record. You kinda trust the folks who you have actually met. You feel your anxiety about your company sort of ease, and the urge to let someone else share the driving for awhile is starting to ramp up.

You start cutting your time with your consultants short. Maybe you don't meet everyone on the team. You get tired of weekly 2-hour status meetings and make it every other week.

Your consultants and their company respond to this. Maybe they relax and schedules start to slip, or maybe they tell their headquarters that they can send over a few extra greenhorns to learn the trade on your project and on your dime. Maybe a prized special-skill consultant gets pulled off to work elsewhere because your company isn't really using him/her.

Maybe they start to push back on your demands by telling you – correctly – that they needed your decision LAST week but you were too busy.

And that's what a **good** consulting company might do. It can be much worse if you accidentally picked a bad company or got some bad people on your team. Imagine getting through half of your project's timeline to discover that not only are milestones being missed but your organization is descending into consultant-induced chaos, and you're still on the hook for that weekly fee.

Much better to buck up now and know that getting outside help didn't mean less work but more, all in the pursuit of a difficult and worthy goal.

Chapter 13

Controlling and evaluating the consulting people

I will say over and over: don't hand over all control of your improvement project to the consultants. That applies hugely to the people they assign to your team.

All consultant companies depend on their people as their main resource for making money. In the same way, the individual consultant people will determine whether a consulting assignment is a success or not. As a result, the consultants will be laser focused on who is staffing your project, but they may have different objectives than you have. You need to be equally focused and reasonably demanding on who will be working in your company: the consultant does not always know best.

One of the smart clients I worked with managed his consultant selection process very well, and appropriately. As the divisional CEO, he was actively involved as we six consultants did our customary four-week business analysis. While he hadn't selected our team members during this initial phase of work, he knew this phase was a demanding short-term chapter that would make each of us and our work quality highly visible. At the close of the analysis, when he was presented with a year-long project proposal, he agreed to it so long as he could select who on our analysis team stayed and who went. He chose wisely, I thought, looking for both the best work qualities and the ability to relate well to his employees and managers. While the consulting company pushed back a bit (disliking the loss of staffing control, among other issues), the client knew he was in the driver's seat. He didn't flinch from politely telling some consultants to go home. He knew how vital it was to have the right people, not just the most convenient people.

(Post script: the project not only was successful in financial and other terms, but was followed with add-on work and a long-term positive client relationship.)

There are several key issues that you as a prospective customer need to be aware of when the consultant is assigning its people to your project.

1. **Inexperienced consultant people may be assigned**. These people may be young, unskilled, unexperienced, or all three. You will be expected to pay for them, perhaps at the same billing rate as other consultants. Too many on one team: you are being short changed and maybe even cheated. One or a small percent will be fine so long as they are true contributors: your consulting company must make that possible while you evaluate their contribution. Just remember that you probably had something to contribute when you were

young or new to a job, too – not least of which being work ethic and ambition.

2. **Some diversity of age and experience** among your consulting people should be present (not to mention gender, ethnicity, etc.). Lack of diversity should be evaluated. Only 28-year-olds with financial services background on your revenue improvement team: a red flag. Also be aware of diversity without value to the team. One tactic I have seen used is injecting a so-called "grey-hair" into the team to give it the appearance of containing at least ONE well-experienced member, without regard to whether that person indeed had that asset.

3. Some (maybe many) **consulting companies have views on people that are not inclusive**: low key or overt racist, sexist, ageist, or other "-ists." Knowing their attitudes on their own people is revealing and may help you select one consulting company over another. Knowing will also help you know if they can summon the best-fit talent for your job. A consulting team of only 30-something white men with monogrammed shirt cuffs is a concern, however talented they might be, especially if your company has a very different mix of employees.

4. **Personality matters**. Incompatible styles at the outset will doom a project. You don't have to like the

consultants but there must be mutual respect and trust to a good degree. Some styles are a no-go anyway, such as autocratic or manipulative. Personality deficits on the team need to be recognized and worked with (maybe one member is a numbers person with lousy people skills: ok only if their work matches their skills). Like all of your people decisions, once isn't forever: keep watching for problems and deal with them if they surface.

5. **People selection isn't forever**. If a consultant starts out ok but then becomes a problem, you should never just live with it. People reviews should be as frequent as financial and progress reviews, and problems with people in a consulting project need to be dealt with faster than with your own people.
6. Almost always **you will not want your consultants to operate alone**, without some of your best people participating, learning, and teaching by their side as fulltime members of a joint team. The selection of your best people could be a book in itself, but in short these will be people with the confidence of senior managers like you, who will both lead and follow the consulting work and keep you informed and involved.

It is fair to ask challenging questions to that consulting salesperson who first darkens your door. It is also vital that challenging questions be asked before you sign up for a business analysis or an improvement project.

Yes, you may get a lot of "happy talk." If your consulting salesperson assures you that they have plenty of, say, black women or bi-lingual Central American professionals, they may be mentally planning an emergency hiring event to get them. Be watchful and get all important assurances in writing. Be clear about consequences for failing to live up to promises. Did I mention in writing? (Expect stalling or resistance, passive or active.)

Controlling your consulting people needs to **start with a good contract** that has received your careful attention. Professional people will respond constructively to the knowledge that you are putting in the time and effort to think the project through. They will also know that their work will be scrutinized and evaluated. You know the squeaky wheel…the reasonably demanding clients are less likely to have funny business pulled on them. Funny business like swapping out great consultants on the introductory analysis for mediocre ones on the project itself. Or stalling when a new project manager is requested, and then requested again, and again.

It is also vital that consequences and corrective procedures be written into any contract. As a client, you should be able to say on Friday that Fred or Mary may not return on

Monday, and that you will no longer pay their fee or expenses after that time. As a client, you should be able to expect a competent replacement very quickly, too.

Of course, I assume that your objective in selecting your consulting team is to get the best people for the job, and that each person earns his or her invoice. The subtext here is that you, no matter your personnel preferences otherwise, will look beyond age, gender, ethnicity, accent, physical appearance, snappy dress, and so on in the quest to get the job done right.

Chapter 14

Controlling and evaluating the consulting schedule

As mentioned previously, it is vital that challenging questions be asked before you sign up for a business analysis or an improvement project.

A written schedule of activities and outcomes is a normal part of any consulting analysis or project. If this seems startling or amazing to your consultant, you need to look for another consultant.

Why so black and white? Well, remember that a good consulting company has done this sort of intervention many times before. They are not making it up from scratch in your case. They have good reasons for what they are doing and a data bank of ideas that regularly bears fruit. They also know how long activities should take once they have an idea of your company's issues and the scope of your problems.

A good consulting company also has critical needs that require careful scheduling and planning. Take staffing, for example. If Maria or Joe is a great consultant, you can be sure that their company wants to make sure they are fully booked. They want to know that in 4 months, they will have Maria or Joe to reassign after they have finished with your project. They will not want Maria or Joe fiddling around aimlessly as your project wanders into its 5th and 6th month with no end in sight.

A good consulting company will also want to manage its costs, especially if it cannot pass them on to you, their client. If there is a fixed time frame for your project with a fixed fee, then overtime costs them money. They manage with project schedules and will also want to manage you and your company with one.

An improvement project or analysis must be guided by a schedule, but **your organization has to be part of setting that up**. Why? Well, your people already have a job and have to accomplish things on separate timelines. Something has to be moved, or de-prioritized, or eliminated, or reassigned. Much better this is done consciously, in advance, rather than seat of pants with arguments or mess-ups later.

Are you the kind of boss who thinks that just laying one more thing on top of the heap is a good way to get things done? Maybe you think your folks are sort of slacking anyway and there is plenty of free time left in their schedule? You might be right, but you also might be wrong. Only your deep involvement with your people in setting up a workable schedule will determine if you are right (which is not so important) and guide your achievement of both project and normal operations goals (which is mighty mighty important).

Getting involved in the details of schedule creation would include:

1. **Listing all the activities in a timeline**. This includes analyzing, doing, and reporting.
2. **Listing all of the people** involved in each activity and time requirements. Project teams typically involve both consultant and client people, often full time for both.
3. **Identifying which activities depend on which other ones** (for example, a perhaps a process has to be analyzed before it is changed).
4. **Identifying the critical path**, which determines the minimum timeline for the project.
5. **Identifying when results will be achieved and how they will be measured**. These become part of the reporting.
6. **Identifying when status update reports will be done** between consultant and you. These should be both written and discussed face to face, with meeting notes taken.
7. **Identifying how schedules will be modified** as circumstances demand.

A few warning signs to work through:

1. If your consultant **dismisses** the need for a written detailed schedule.
2. If the schedule offered by the consultant is **vague** and boiler-plate.
3. If the consultant **pushes back** on you being involved in setting the schedule and contributing to its details.
4. If there are **no timeframes** for accomplishment.
5. If the process of discussing schedule feels like **being dictated to** versus being collaborated with.

Chapter 15

Controlling and evaluating the consulting cost

On many consulting projects, two kinds of bills will be presented by your consultant: fees and expenses. The consulting contract must deal in detail with both, and both must be managed frequently and closely.

Consulting fees

Fees for an engagement can be either **fixed or variable**. Fixed fees would be tied to a given scope of work with a time schedule and expected outcomes. Variable fees might be daily or hourly, and would be tied to a specific goal.

For example, a fixed fee project might be to improve sales revenues by 20% in 12 months by creating and implementing a customer contact and sales management system.

- Once the schedule and staffing are agreed to, a fixed fee is calculated to be billed over the life of the project.
- The fee may be calculated and billed per week, or as the sum of daily billing rates per consultant, or by other means.
- If the project over-ran the total agreed dollar fee, then the contract must have language to deal with what

happens next. Maybe no dollar over-runs will be paid for under any circumstances, or maybe there are some situations where an over-run is paid for.

- There also would need to be provisions for under-runs, which is really important, for instance, if the consultant reduces their staffing more than contracted for.

A variable fee consultant engagement might be one where an outcome is needed, even if it takes more time than might be estimated. For instance, if consultants were hired to help solve a process problem that resulted in a product recall, the urgency and critical nature of the problem might be enough to let you forego some control over the total price tag. Only some control should be relaxed, however, and oversight and review are at least as important as with fixed fee contracts.

If you have a worrier on your staff somewhere, he or she can help create a contract with your consultant that anticipates the unexpected and answers each with clear and specific actionable items. For instance:

- What control over individual consultants and their fees do you need?
- Do you understand the billing method, or is there too much vagueness to hold your consultants accountable?

- What if the best individual on their team is yanked off and replaced by a greenhorn but the billing rate is the same?
- What if you are billed for a consultant who wasn't actually working that week?
- Should you be billed for 5 days when consultants leave before noon on Fridays?

Expenses

Many consulting engagements include some allowable categories of expense for the consulting team. For instance, out of town people might get reimbursed for reasonable travel expenses, maybe daily food allowances, and modest job-related costs like specialized safety equipment. A good contract will specify perhaps that sales or management visits by non-project-team members are not cost-reimbursable, and list other non-reimbursable expenses if that makes sense.

Accountability by routine expense report review should also be part of the contract, and expense reports should indeed be regularly reviewed. One category of cost – travel – should be well managed for cost by the consulting company, with certain possible abuses like business class travel being listed as non-reimbursable.

If a project is of long duration, your company may want to take an active role in reducing expenses. For instance, your company may have a corporate rate at a hotel, or you may have a travel department who can assist in reducing prices. Your company may be able to rent apartments that are less costly than hotels, and supply company cars rather than have consultants rent cars.

The flip side of managing cost is managing consultant time. Anything you can do to make each consulting minute count will improve outcomes and possibly reduce the cost of doing so. And managing time also requires your hands-on attention.

Chapter 16

Controlling and evaluating the project outcome

You would think that, after 4 or 6 weeks of an in-depth analysis and 5 weeks of negotiation and contract-wrangling, both consultant and client would have a clear idea of what an improvement project would involve and include.

But no.

To deal with inevitable issues of understanding and clarity, I learned to use a useful technique called the "expectation exchange." This technique was designed because, on Project Day 1, there were plenty of misconceptions about what was about to happen and what the goals of a project were.

During this exchange, both the key client managers and the consultant(s) on the project would list their expectations of the project and their counterparts. A client manager might say that they expected to find out which products needed to be discontinued, and the consultant might counter with "No, our mission is to work with you to increase revenues from the products you currently sell." A consultant might say they expected at least 10 days in the field with 10 different field service representatives, and the service manager might find this added work to be a complete surprise.

This is part of expectation and outcome control: know what the project is supposed to accomplish and what is needed to get there. The other important part: track to be sure you are achieving those goals, and getting them on time per your schedule.

One effective way to manage a project's outcomes (and costs, people, and schedule) is a weekly review meeting between you, appropriate key people of yours, and the consultant manager. A weekly meeting means less overwhelming information, quicker problem solving, and immediate two-way feedback. Also, if you are paying a weekly bill, it is nice to match results to the invoice, especially if you have a Board to report to.

A good weekly meeting is not when the consultant is checking his/her watch for that run to the airport. Better a Thursday, which allows another day or so that same week to address action plans before problems fester.

A good weekly meeting includes a two-way detailed review of the project schedule (maybe a Gantt chart), a clear reporting of successes and issues, and an explicit action plan going forward.

As the client, you have a right to see the results promised in your contract if you have held up your end. You also have a responsibility to look for problems in that obligation early. It is possible to finish a project schedule and pay all the fees and not achieve your expected results…and then what? Should you have smelled danger earlier? Should you have intervened? Were you warned? Are you in a worse position now than before you started?

This is why you must control the achievement of outcomes, because a project on auto pilot can fail completely, while costing a ton, and while poisoning your company morale.

Chapter 17

Making it work through mutual respect

Mutual respect is an irreplaceable ingredient for a successful consulting project.

Disrespect can be voiced, and unvoiced disrespect will leak out in actions. Here's what disrespect might look like.

Consultant to client:

- Words to the effect: "Step aside, little people, and let us show you how it is done."
- Words like "you have no idea" or "You're wrong" or "if you just think about it…"
- Actions like ignoring input from people specifically pointed to by the client, or failing to frequently communicate and solicit input.
- Actions like "implementing with both feet:" using force, autocratic methods, etc. versus collaboration.

Client to consultant:

- Words like "is this your first job after school?" and "Do you have any idea…?"
- Actions like frequent meeting cancellations or short inattentive meetings.

- Actions that are dismissive towards individuals.

Respect is the lubricant of positive human relations.

- Respect opens ears.
- Respect increases openness to change.
- Respect creates a learning environment.
- Respect creates likeability, which leads to a cascade of positive interactions between people.

Lack of respect allows suspicion, distrust, and unproductive relationships to flourish. Lack of respect creates an emotional response that blocks input and, thus, change.

You, your folks at all levels, and consultants all need to show respect, although the consultant as the guest and the paid professional has a higher burden.

The best CONSULTANTS would use these techniques:

1. Listen. Take notes when listening. Make direct eye contact and ask clarifying and follow-up questions. Avoid challenging before understanding.
2. Freely provide valuable information. Offer clarification on what is being done and why to each person they work with. Offer anecdotes of similar situations in other companies and parallels to your company. Demystify the consulting process.

3. Acknowledge people. Greet people while meeting their eyes, especially non-management people, who may be used to being overlooked. Go out of the way to ask open ended opinion questions of everyone, like "what most needs improvement in your department?"
4. Assume competence and intelligence in everyone. Frame questions and provide input with that in mind.
5. Provide respect to those least likely to get or expect it, not just those in power.
6. Truly believe that they as the consultant can learn from the client, and find out exactly how. Proactively mine the company for ideas, opinions, feedback, suggestions, comparisons with other clients, etc. Fight defensiveness if challenged by company people. Admit error if it occurs.
7. Adapt communication styles and methods to best help the company. In particular, manage how criticism and suggestions for change can be delivered to be most acceptable and useful.

Respect from company people towards the consultant is a bit different. As both the host and the party being criticized and corrected, there may be situations where even politeness seems a challenge. However, if you and your fellow company employees work with the consultants as valued professionals, they will (being human) do better work for you.

The respectful CLIENT would:

1. Listen. Take notes when listening. Make direct eye contact and ask clarifying and follow up questions. Avoid challenging before understanding.

2. Freely provide valuable information. Offer clarification on what is wrong and right about your company's situation. Look to fill in critical information gaps the consultant may have. Help your consultant be effective.

3. Assume competence and intelligence in every consultant on the project. Frame questions and provide input with that in mind.

4. Provide respect to those least likely to get or expect it, not just those in power.

5. Truly believe that you can learn from the consultant, and find out exactly how. Proactively mine the consultant for ideas, opinions, feedback, suggestions, comparisons with other clients, etc. Fight defensiveness if challenged or questioned. Admit error if that is appropriate or useful to progress.

6. Adapt communication styles and methods to best help the company. Add or adapt to create a continuously improving culture.

7. Forgive errors by your consultant if they are corrected properly.

Chapter 18

Making it fail, accidentally or on purpose

Maybe you were informed one day – to your complete surprise – by your boss or your Board that a consultant would be hired to work with your team, in your own sandbox. Boy, are you pissed.

Or maybe it's not you but your management team that is surprised and pissed.

So, you, or they, decide to make these arrogant twits' lives hell, since punishing your/their management directly is pretty much a non-starter. Payback might include passive resistance, canceling meetings, failing to meet commitments, withholding information, saying nasty things to peers and boss(es), and so on.

If you cannot deal effectively with such obstructionist behavior, then save your organization the cash and pain and just don't hire a consultant. Your organization can do badly enough on its own, with less aggravation. Why bring in an outsider with an agenda of improvement, give your people hope of positive change, and then appall them with more of the usual?

A manager saddled with a consultant could conceivably choose to see the situation positively: he/she/they were given another resource with which to work, just like an accountant or a research scientist. However, even if true, this can be a very difficult thing to do. Emotional needs, like self-protection and ego, are involved.

A great deal has been written about emotional issues within organizations and how they affect lives and companies: I won't even try to summarize. Most importantly, however: emotional needs and issues should not be overlooked, downplayed, or ignored. We can't wish away our human traits when they become troublesome or inconvenient.

Politics are always a part of any organization that has people in it. Human drives for power, prestige, security, respect, and so on will always be present. These needs have to be identified and dealt with to pave a path for an effective consulting effort. Otherwise, insecurity, resentment, and other toxins will breed and fester, impeding or destroying the effort.

A constructive leader will recognize the ego-crushing potential of a consulting project and deal with it head on. Most importantly, the best people need to know that they are hugely valued and not less so than these outsiders. **Use more than words**: get them involved in the project and ask for their ideas. The more damaging course would be that you choose to under-communicate and under-encourage and imply by your words and deeds that your staff are, in fact, lacking and losing, and watch the project suffer accordingly.

A constructive leader should also explore the ego-bruising possibility that consultants are being hired due in part to their own inability to hire/fire the right people, train their people, provide leadership in process and product, and a zillion other possibilities. In other words: a good leader will look for his/her own deficits and determine that they will also need to be addressed as part of the improvement project.

An improvement project is about more than objective business measures, but also about people, culture, and communication. As a leader, you are essential to meeting those more subjective needs in addition to the objective ones. On the other hand, if you think a performance improvement consultant should just be pointed, wound up, and let loose on their own, you are going to be very disappointed.

Both your organization and your consultant need to be managed, assisted, supported and given every opportunity to do their best work.

If not…

Things you can DO wrong to make things GO wrong include:

1. Failing to clarify performance expectations in writing, mutually agreed.
2. Not addressing problems of employee obstruction in constructive ways.
3. Telling your people that the consultant is here as a result of their failings.
4. Not addressing employee fears proactively and quickly, especially job security and the effects of changes.
5. Not having frequent progress meetings with consultants and key employees.
6. Not being open to hearing and dealing with problems.
7. Not dealing with problem consultants.
8. Not knowing your consultants individually.
9. Not being open to course corrections.
10. Not communicating with managers or a Board senior to you. (Expectations can be surprisingly off target without communication.)
11. Allowing yourself to be surprised, often by under-communication.
12. Being the Lone Ranger managing the project yourself, without the aid and advice of your key people.

13. Failing to keep evaluating course headings, progress, satisfaction, and challenges.
14. Insisting that your business is so unique that the people/process/product/strategy ideas and improvements from an outsider could not possibly apply, and blocking those efforts.

And then, what could happen?

The worst case: your company is poorer, the project does not complete or does not achieve expected results, your people are stressed, overworked, and frustrated, and your senior leadership is so upset that scapegoats will be dealt with harshly.

If you are seriously considering the consulting route, it is vital to know in advance **that it is not a purchase so much as an adoption**. Like a puppy from the shelter, you pay a fee, and bring home a bundle of possibilities. You keep spending money on upkeep in order to gain a treasured new member of the family. However, if you don't train, walk, or socialize it, your hoped-for love muffin will be an undisciplined, troublesome, and expensive destructive force. And like a bad puppy, a poor consulting experience will be mostly your own doing.

Chapter 19

Maybe you need – but can't use – a consultant

You have read, so far, that consultants can add value and, especially, inject some important skills and knowledge into an organization faster than just figuring it all out on your own.

However, consulting is no substitute for the right people, especially the right leadership and management people. In fact, without good leaders, the consulting work will not stick long term.

And even good consulting can be applied to the wrong situations and either be wasted or create more problems.

Some situations where you should not hire consultants include:

1. Hiring an organizational development consultant when the company urgently needs to focus on quality and a shrinking market.
2. Hiring a strategy consultant when the company cannot execute.
3. Hiring a six-sigma consultant when the company is not even a two-sigma one.

4. Hiring team building or similar human relations consultants because senior leadership thinks there is a morale problem.
5. When you are unable or unwilling to devote the time of some of the best employees to an improvement project.
6. When you are unable or unwilling to work harder than you already are during the life of the project.
7. When you are unable or unwilling to do things you usually avoid, like developing and firing people, at every level.

Hiring a consultant under any of these circumstances can be worse than nothing. It can crush your best people with false hope, all while wasting time and money.

If you cannot commit to the time, work, stress, behavior changes, and discomfort, then don't bother with a consultant.

To some degree, working successfully with a consultant and then not following through with ongoing change and improvements can also be a long-term negative, especially for your best people. The hope and enthusiasm sparked in those folks by finally being listened to, being part of something excellent, and seeing a brighter personal and company future can lead to greater disappointment and unhappiness if improvements were fleeting and never repeated. I saw this in defense contractors, for instance, who would want to look good for an admiral's visit but who reverted back to standard practice shortly afterwards. Our consulting projects in these firms were met with cynicism and lip service, and improvements did not stick even medium term.

Section C: Moving On

Chapter 20

Letting your consultants go

You had better learn how to let your consultants go, or you're not progressing, and you are spending too much money in the meantime.

Consultants are jump-starters and butt-kickers, not lifelong addictions. If you want the skills full time, hire people (even those consultants), but you need to learn jump-starting and butt-kicking yourselves.

Some very large companies have maintained long term consulting relationships for years. There might be a good cost/benefit, but I suspect instead that it is a way to either offset management that hasn't learned enough to keep the ball rolling, or to provide a pool of super competent people who can be pointed at problems and who can also be fired at will and kept off the headcount.

Don't do it. Get the benefit and move on, using what has been learned to keep moving forward.

As a consultant, I would help sell "extension" projects that followed after the first improvement project ended. These did sell after a successful first outcome, because many large companies have divisions that are not able to learn from each other. Maybe one extension would be good for both client and consultant, but more than one may say that the company isn't doing what it should to learn the change process for itself.

Don't be that company. All the consulting stuff can be learned.

Chapter 21

If all goes well

Believe it or not, you and your organization may end up enjoying the process of working with a consultant or a consulting group.

Here are some positive outcomes of a good project:

1. The people in your organization who thrive on achievement will, well, thrive, and bring better ongoing results.
2. Many of the best people will have breakthrough thinking experiences, which can truly re-energize.
3. People will learn things, often interesting things, that improve their work life. They may experience the pleasure of being asked to advise and design.
4. If done correctly, people at all levels in the company will believe that the company is serious about change and improvement. This knowledge will reduce energy-sapping cynicism.
5. The sense of futility, desperation, frustration, or confusion will lessen, and this will reduce the anxiety and loss of energy that comes with such feelings.

6. Nothing binds a group of people together like overcoming shared obstacles. Teamwork and morale will improve.
7. Those who thrive on challenge and some excitement at work have the deadline and results driven consulting project to drive them. It can be something to look forward to every day.
8. A consulting project is a productive diversion that sparks interest and focus just by its non-routine nature.
9. A consulting project may highlight high potential people who otherwise were hidden from view.
10. A consulting project may create inter-department and inter-discipline cooperation and teamwork that serves as a stronger foundation for the future.

Chapter 22

Breaking the habit

For those of you who are opposed to using consultants at all, you may feel vindicated when I tell you that consultants should not be constantly hired to fix the same kinds of problems over and over. Change management and process improvement are far too important skills to not have within your company.

If you found it useful to have a consultant around, you should also find it useful to learn their skills and let them go.

Consulting needs to be outgrown, like school, not made permanent, like a pacemaker. However, like any change, it takes more than a hearty "gotta do it" to make it happen.

As you evaluate how well equipped your company is becoming to carry on without outside help, consider this:

1. Change takes effort and energy. Have you created a way to generate, channel and encourage change energy in your company?

2. Continuous improvement takes never-ending analysis and change. What have you put in place that is

different from before to support these critical and resource-consuming activities?

Even more specifically:

1. Do you have any fulltime change leader(s)? Some organizations create a Continuous Improvement Manager with senior status and access to senior management. Six Sigma and similar programs often do this, to continuously fuel and prod change, and gain top level support for it.

2. Do you have skilled people who know how to create ideas, get input, gain support, and implement change? For example, do you have skilled meeting facilitators, finance people who know how to create scorecards, ongoing employee activities geared to continuous improvement?

3. Have you included in your consulting project requirements that your consulting professionals set up a post-project continuous improvement organization, or at least write a report detailing recommendations for doing so?

On the last day of your consulting project, your organization should look and behave differently than at the outset. Your people will probably fall into two camps on this: one which hopes the positive change will continue, or even accelerate, and one which is hoping that it all will go away and leave them in peace. Your organization needs to harness the first group's hopes and skills. Your change agents and leaders will come from that group.

If the project went well and your company improved and grew its collective skills, your best people's morale will improve. You may even see excitement, and you may discover in your staff skills and energy you never knew existed. Your ability to keep the momentum going will keep those positive feelings and outcomes working well into the future.

Section D: Appendix

Appendix 1

Lessons learned from the author's consulting experience

I was hired as a staff consultant for United Research Corp. in 1983. This was a midsized consulting company, boasting approximately 200 professionals. The company did have many very intelligent, driven, hard-working, educated, and experienced pros who served their clients well.

The five years I spent with this company were transformational for me. United Research Corp. (URC) was worlds different from the large public companies I had previously worked for. Many of the differences were very positive ones, focused on excellence.

Here are a few of those positive features that made me a strong supporter of good consulting (and good management) forever after:

1. URC had explicit, **written values and a mission**, which focused on excellence and serving the customer.
2. URC's CEO genuinely **lived the values** and rigorously enforced them in his people and processes.
3. URC was **organized and systematic** in its work. It had written manuals on how to do business analyses and improvement projects. Its consultants were tasked to

write how-to white papers on improving different business processes, like machinery maintenance or power line inspections or cable TV service phone bank methods. It had a library for its internal guides and a librarian. Managers had to write weekly reports for HQ review, and a final report to leave with the client. It had an internal quality assurance department and an audit process for ongoing projects.

4. URC focused on **continuously improving** its methods and teaching its consultants these new methods.
5. URC **recognized merit and accomplishment** in its consultants, and removed professionals who didn't measure up.
6. URC **focused on the fundamentals** of running a healthy business: people, process, strategy, tactics. It usually merged worthwhile parts of management fads into its basic fundamental approaches.
7. URC **appreciated and cultivated** its clients and their people, as shown by its value for the "Theory Y" management style over "Theory X." (Simplistically, carrot versus stick, respect versus contempt.)
8. URC **focused on implementation** over report writing; actual results over theoretical future opportunities.

Of course, URC wasn't perfect, and the various consulting sins I have discussed here have been those I saw firsthand. However, its style and standards lead to positive results with many clients, and fostered many years of successful follow-on business.

I was privileged to work with clients like General Motors, Kodak, DuPont, The Southern Company, McDonnell Douglas Astronautics, Miller Brewing, Cablevision, Carrier, Raytheon, AT&T/Bell Labs, and others, often as project manager. Every company taught me something new about best practices and business challenges, while also showing how every business shared commonalities that could be leveraged from one project to the next ones.

Here are some of those lessons learned from my client experiences.

1. **Companies are often very much like other companies** in which problems they have and why. In particular, as long as companies keep hiring people, they will always have people problems. In addition, it is common to find significant gaps in training and documentation for training. Frequently cost accounting is not accurate or detailed enough to use for rapid and effective product or service decisions. Management reporting on critical business indicators is often lacking at all levels.

2. **Business systems can be – and have been – systematically studied** and improved. Practices that are currently done by seat of the pants in any business can be made efficient and effective using proven methods. Clients will often add to the consultant's list of effective systems even while some other systems of theirs are being upgraded with consulting help.

3. Many clients will **claim they have the best people**. However, many will not have the knowledge to know what "best people" look like, or how it is management's job to hire and train and support employees to make them the "best." And so they do NOT, in fact have the best people.

4. Many client companies are **uncomfortable with confronting** their consultants about people or processes they are unhappy about. When they do, however, in a respectful way, they get better outcomes.

5. The **best consulting experiences are with business-smart, reasonably demanding and non-ego-threatened clients**. These provided the most amazing transformations, with the highest likelihood of "sticking." The clients in these cases were involved enough to have real expectations, knowledgeable enough to know that some issues needed attention, and self-assured enough to know that help was a pathway to

larger successes they could both share in and take credit for.

6. **The consultant role will have power that most employee roles will never have**. The power is in being listened to, being assumed worth listening to, and in having less fear in speaking.

7. Many companies struggle with – or completely **fail at – firing or correcting underperforming people** at every level. This is extremely corrosive to a company and the majority of its good people. It can be a great gift to a client to set up a way to change this situation. However, when the underperforming problem shows up within senior management, the consultant may have no ability to affect the situation, and may decide to settle for being a permanent sidekick with shorter term improvements and a reliable consulting income stream.

8. The most valuable skills as a consulting project manager start with and rely upon **good people treatment**: showing respect, and listening to everyone (including the painful, even whiney, types). When you listen, you get more information. When you deal respectfully, people don't avoid, obstruct, or clam up as much. All of this leads to results.

9. Many companies have no idea that they should have a **habit of continuous improvement** that involves all

workers and managers. For these companies, all improvements become projects: added work, not normal work. The energy required to keep constantly starting and managing projects in this extraordinary model becomes exhausting and inevitably inadequate. What's more, many items that could have been solved get worse with time; opportunities can also get lost if not seized quickly.

10. The world is full of **mediocre companies making a profit**. It's amazing how many organizations are financially OK, even with glaring product, customer, and employee inadequacies that are not being addressed. This type of company can benefit significantly from consulting but may be the most resistant to it.

11. **Every company has something of value to teach its consultant**. Many times something is done very well somewhere within the company. Sometimes there are lessons on how not to be successful. Other times there are strategic or tactical ideas that enrich an understanding of how businesses and people work. All are gifts.

12. A company, after a successful project, may have a new appreciation for the **benefits of continuous improvement** and how much skill and energy is

required to keep that process going. Sometimes a company will want to hire a particularly effective and good-fit consultant. This can be a win-win if managed in an upfront way.

Appendix 2

Types of consultants

One complexity in writing this book was in the definition of "consultant," and its different uses in different industries.

Some managers I have met recoiled with disgust when I used the word "consultant," yet they regularly and effectively purchased consulting services under different terms.

The biggest difference between management/business improvement consultants and many of these other consultants is the clear and narrow scope of the latter. You, the client, understand what a packaging line consultant is being hired to do, and have some clear ideas of what their expected outcome and cost will be. A management consultant, however…maybe not.

An important lesson then: **get the same comfort with scope, objectives, and cost with the more unfamiliar business consultant**.

You may be familiar with many consultant types, such as:

1. The kind that is technically focused, like packaging consultants, or production equipment experts, or tax experts, or manufacturing engineer experts, or public relations experts.

2. The kind that focuses on people issues: training, hiring, morale, succession planning, skill building, and so on.
3. Crisis or special circumstance consultants, like media, legal, regulatory, or legislative consultants.
4. The kind that focuses on industry issues, like how to compete better in food distribution.
5. The kind that focuses on being a close advisor to the senior leader or leadership team for various items.
6. Coach consultants, who focus on individuals in the management team, advising on personal style, specific skills, etc.
7. The kind that specializes in the "big picture," such as strategy consultants. They may advise reorganizations, or different product line focus or such high-level stuff. These services may or may not include implementation.
8. The kind that communicates mostly one way (they ask, you answer) and then they write a report on results.
9. The kind that do #8 and also tell you what needs to be fixed, but not how.
10. The kind focused on process improvement, which may or may not include people and strategy.
11. All of the above, but focusing on only large, or medium, or small, or startup businesses.

Your objective in hiring consultants and contractors is to meet occasional needs demanding high and/or specific skills and added people hours. Consultants are contractors, but are expected to be expert, self-directed contractors, often with a project focus. Projects are usually supposed to end sometime in the foreseeable future, leaving a more capable company ready to keep up the momentum.

Final words

This book's focus is to be a quick but thorough guide to facilitate understanding and decision making. That means it is long on lists, short on stories. Stories, however, can communicate ideas in a uniquely effective way.

For more stories in greater depth, I highly recommend one storybook about consulting: Dangerous Company: Management Consultants and the Businesses They Save and Ruin by James O'Shea and Charles Madigan, 1998. Never mind the age of the book and often the obsolescence of key players: some lessons are timeless. In particular, Chapter 4 on Sears and its CEO Arthur Martinez during the 1990's is a good illustration on how to use consultants effectively, along with managing them even more effectively.

Another short book worth a look:

Selecting and Working with Consultants: A Guide for Clients by Thomas J. Ucko, Crisp Publications, Inc., Los Altos CA, 1990. This is a workbook style book with exercises and practical suggestions.

I can be contacted by

- Email: nancyk@plsconsulting.com
- Website at www.plsconsulting.com
- LinkedIn www.linkedin.com/in/nancykrug1

I welcome your comments, experiences, ideas, and success stories.

www.ingramcontent.com/pod-product-compliance
Lightning Source LLC
LaVergne TN
LVHW020643100826
845148LV00012B/2314

* 9 7 8 1 7 3 5 4 7 5 7 1 4 *